All About Heat

By Lisa Trumbauer

Consultants
David Larwa
National Science Consultant

Nanci R. Vargus, Ed.D.
Assistant Professor of Literacy
University of Indianapolis
Indianapolis, Indiana

Children's Press®
A Division of Scholastic Inc.
New York   Toronto   London   Auckland   Sydney
Mexico City   New Delhi   Hong Kong
Danbury, Connecticut

Designer: Herman Adler Design
Photo Researcher: Caroline Anderson
The photo on the cover shows a teapot over a gas range.

Library of Congress Cataloging-in-Publication Data

Trumbauer, Lisa, 1963-
  All about heat / by Lisa Trumbauer.
     p. cm. — (Rookie read-about science)
Includes index.
Summary: An introduction to the sources and characteristics of heat.
  ISBN 0-516-23608-3 (lib. bdg.)   0-516-25846-X (pbk.)
  1. Heat—Juvenile literature. [1. Heat.] I. Title. II. Series.
  QC256.T78 2003
  536—dc22

                                    2003019065

CHILDREN'S PRESS, and ROOKIE READ-ABOUT®,
and associated logos are trademarks and or registered trademarks
of Scholastic Library Publishing. SCHOLASTIC and associated logos
are trademarks and or registered trademarks of Scholastic Inc.

1 2 3 4 5 6 7 8 9 10 R 13 12 11 10 09 08 07 06 05 04

Close your eyes and lift
your face to the sun.
What do you feel?

You feel heat.

The sun is hot.
It warms the earth.

The sun makes heat.

A fire in a fireplace is hot.
It warms the room.

Fire gives off heat.

Heat is energy moving
from one thing to another.

On a warm day, energy
from the sun warms the
air. You can wear light
clothing.

9

Step into the shade. The air here is cool. The tree blocks the sun's energy.

Heat goes from hot things
to cold things.

Lick an ice cream cone.

The heat from your tongue
warms the ice cream. The
ice cream melts.

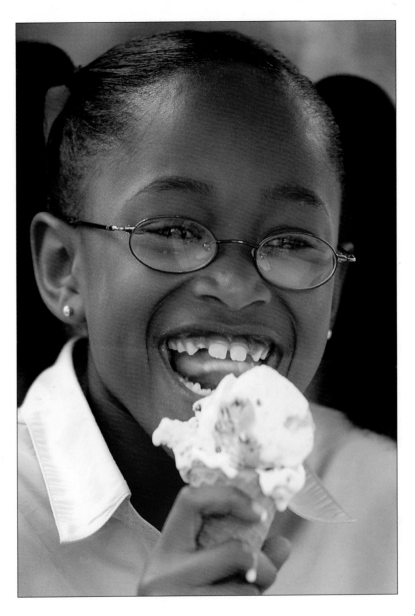

When heat moves from a
hot thing to a colder thing,
the hot thing cools down.

Go into the water on a
warm day at the beach.

The heat moves from
your body to the water.
This cools you down.

We use heat to cook.
Charcoal burns in a grill.
This makes heat.

Charcoal

The heat from the charcoal cooks the food.

Mix up some cookies and put them in the oven.

The oven makes heat. The heat cooks the cookies.

Now you have a tasty treat.

We use a tool called
a thermometer to
measure heat.

The amount of heat is
called the temperature
(TEM-pur-uh-chur).

One of the hottest places on Earth is a desert. The temperature can be more than 100 degrees.

24

A warm, sunny day is about 80 degrees. You can feel the sun's heat.

You can feel the sun's energy on a cold day, too. The sun's energy can melt the snow and ice.

Heat is warm.
Heat is energy.
Can you feel the heat?

Words You Know

charcoal

desert

grill

thermometer

Index

About the Author

Lisa Trumbauer has written a dozen books about the physical sciences and dozens more about other branches of science. She has also edited science programs for teachers of young children. Lisa lives in New Jersey with one dog, two cats, and her husband, Dave.

Photo Credits

Photographs © 2004: Corbis Images: 9 (John Henley), 7 (Greg Nikas), 14 (David Samuel Robbins), 5 (Royalty-Free); Dembinsky Photo Assoc.: 6 (Stephen Graham), 23, 30, 30 bottom (Scott T. Smith), 20 (Aaron Haupt); Photo Researchers/Aaron Haupt, NY: 31 bottom; PhotoEdit: 19 (Michael Newman), 24 (Vicki Silbert), 10, 13 (David Young-Wolff); PictureQuest/Ron Chapple/Thinkstock: cover; The Image Works: 27 (Skip O'Rourke), 16, 31 top (Rhoda Sidney); Visuals Unlimited: 28 (Mark E. Gibson), 3 (Jeff Greenberg), 17, 30 top (Laura Martin).